I0764360

Upcycling Paumanok

UPCYCLING PAUMANOK

Poems by

Ned Balbo

Measure Press
Evansville, Indiana

Printed in the United States of America
First Edition

The text of this book is composed in Baskerville.
Composition by R.G.
Manufacturing by Ingram.

Balbo, Ned
Upcycling Paumanok / by Ned Balbo — 1st ed.

ISBN-13: 978-1-939574-15-2
ISBN-10: 1-939574-15-3
Library of Congress Control Number: 2016908617

Epigraph sources:

Josephine Jacobsen, "The Planet," *In the Crevice of Time* (Johns Hopkins: 1995).

Philip Larkin, "Going, Going," *High Windows* (Farrar, Straus and Giroux: 1974).

Louise Bogan, "After the Persian," *The Blue Estuaries* (Ecco: 1977).

Measure Press
526 S. Lincoln Park Dr.
Evansville, IN 47714
http://www.measurepress.com/measure/

Acknowledgments

The author wishes to thank the editors of the publications in which these poems have appeared, sometimes in slightly different form.

Angle: "Stray Crow"
Archaeopteryx: "A Parable of Flight," "For Jacob Kurtzberg"
Baltimore Review: "Dark Horse"
The Common: "Upcycling Paumanok"
The Dark Horse: "Return from Slumberland"
Italian Americana: "The Woods"
Notre Dame Review: "Times Square Post Cards" 1, 3, and 6
Per Contra: "Cosmology Past Midnight in Midsummer"
Potomac Review: "Ouija for Beginners"
Raintown Review: "Breakthrough"
River Styx: "Green Ghost"
Rondeau Roundup: "Rondel for a Timepiece Not Yet Obsolete"
Studio: "Blue Panther," "The Ex-Friends"
Truck: "Suicide of an Old Man"
Valparaiso Poetry Review: "On Goodbyes," "For My Step-Daughter, Who Missed the Apparition," "Dead Man Walking"
Young Adult Review Network (YARN): "Ante Meridiem"

Versions of the following poems first appeared in the chapbook *Something Must Happen* (Finishing Line Press): "Snow in Baghdad," "Actors Talking While They Drive," "Aerial Views of Levittown," "A Nonsense Name," "A Dog and a Wolf," "Times Square Post Cards" (2, 4, and 5), "Already Seen/Always Seen," "Holy Wars for Us," "For the Next-to-Last Survivor."

I'm grateful that several poems found homes in anthologies or other forums, including the following:

"For Jacob Kurtzberg": *Drawn to Marvel: Poems from the Comic Books* (Minor Arcana Press), edited by Bryan D. Dietrich and Marta Ferguson; *Poet of the Month* online anthology (Terri Witek, curator).

"Dead Man Walking": *Poetry Ireland Review* special issue "Name and Nature: 'Who Do You Say I Am?'"
"A Parable of Flight": *Poet of the Month* online anthology.
"Ouija for Beginners": *Potomac Review* special issue "Best of the 50."
"Snow in Baghdad" and "Holy Wars for Us": *The Art of Peace* (Peace Day chapbook anthology, Curran Center for Catholic Studies), edited by Angela Alaimo O'Donnell.
"On Goodbyes": *Valparaiso Poetry Review* editor's blog "One Poet's Notes" (Poem of the Week).

"Snow in Baghdad," "Dead Man Walking" and "For My Step-Daughter, Who Missed the Apparition" were finalists for the Pirate's Alley Faulkner Society poetry award.

I want to extend thanks to the Hyla Brook Poets, Powow River Poets, Maryland State Arts Council, Vermont Studio Center, Virginia Center for the Creative Arts, West Chester University Poetry Conference, and Iowa State University for welcome support.

Among those who offered invaluable encouragement or suggestions during the period when these poems were being written are Dick Allen, Kim Bridgford, Edward Byrne, Dana Gioia, Sam Gwynn, Andrew Hudgins, Mark Jarman, Leah and Kevin Maines, Charles Martin, Angela Alaimo O'Donnell, V. Penelope Pelizzon, David Rothman, Dean Smith, Elizabeth Spires, Daniel Tobin, Lew Turco, Lesley Wheeler, and David Yezzi.

Thanks to composer Alex Nohai-Seaman for using "Holy Wars for Us" as the text for the first movement of his art song cycle *Warbook*.

For last-minute help and critical insight on "Time Square Post Cards," thanks to G. Scott Allen and Mark Osteen.

Special thanks to longtime colleagues Kathleen Forni, Barbara Mallonee, Brian Murray, and Mark Osteen.

For kindness long remembered, thank you to my teachers: Walter Belinsky, Frank Carnese, Art Freed, Marilyn Flamberg, Michael Garramone, Ross Herzog, Castor Howard, and Gail Inzerillo-Latella.

I'm deeply grateful to Rob Griffith and Paul Bone for editorial guidance and support.

With love and thanks to Jane, partner in life and poetry.

CONTENTS

1.

2.

3.

1.

... a blue sky carrying clouds;
and water, water: the innocent planet,
shining and shining.
— Josephine Jacobsen

Cosmology Past Midnight in Midsummer

A swimming pool in darkness cannot hold
the sky's starlit immensity, but two,
sleepless together, can't resist the view —
cicadas surge. No guard's on watch tonight.
Above them, far from artificial light,
the stars look brighter, infinite, and cold.
The water doesn't move. Two click the frames
of chairs that let them lie back and look up —
the constellations! Neither knows their names
so they make up a few. But when they stop,
the stars persist, undaunted. Does the sky —
dust-scattered, black — change imperceptibly
above their gaze? They almost think it does,
despite its depths: remote, mysterious.

Ouija for Beginners

Ouija knows all the answers. Weird and mysterious.
Surpasses, in its unique results, mind reading,
clairvoyance, and second sight.

The Ouija Board requires two believers
seeking favors

of the spirits. As above, so below —
the planchette window

inches toward a numeral or letter.
With a shudder,

characters accrue to words, or names,
random sums

to dates — lost birthdays, anniversaries —
at which we freeze

in recognition, cold hands quivering,
our wavering

connection to the dead a revelation.
Will a vision

welcome us, tonight, into the dark?
What else might lurk

beyond the world we let ourselves behold?
Forget the old

apocrypha of how the term was coined —
that two words joined,

to form a double "Yes" in French and German;
learn to listen

for assent, refusal in the silence —
sift the nonsense

mixed with truths half-spelled out on the board
where all you've heard,

or dreaded, lies encoded. Patience, now:
the dead are slow:

they've all eternity before they nudge
the planchette-edge

through hands you thought were yours, quite powerless,
to rest on *Yes*,

or, just as easily, *No*.... Unless it's you
who move it, too.

Actors Talking While They Drive

It always happens in the course
of chase, escape, or dialogue:
some actor, steering past the shores
of traffic, smiles with a shrug
then launches into monologue,
eyes straying from the road. I watch,
call out, *Look straight ahead*, a plague
of fear descending with a touch.

Something must happen; that's the source
of all suspense. The town's main drag,
innocuous, slips past, bright colors
bearing new risks, new intrigue,
plot-twists that viewers catalogue
at every turn. Or else the clutch
is just a clutch: speed through the fog.
Don't talk when fear extends its touch!

When no one crashes, is it worse?
The soundtrack rises with its fugue
of squeals and sawed-on strings, the doors
locked tight, the passenger in league
with cop, ex-lover, friend? It's vague,
but no one likes the driver much.
The passenger fights off fatigue,
feigns interest. Fear extends its touch.

Stop talking — watch the road! One tug
back from the brink is theirs. Or such
swift carnage it's mere epilogue
to fear's release and final touch.

The *Poseidon*, Capsized

On seeing The Poseidon Adventure, *March 1973*

Huddled in the dark with Miriam —
that's Mimi, my first girlfriend — on a field trip
to the movies for East Junior High's
eighth-graders, and a lucky few in ninth,
I looked up, rapt, the pre-multiplex screen
all water churned by one enormous wave
that rolled supremely toward the ill-starred ship
where Carol Lynley lip-synched words of comfort
for tuxedoed drunks on New Year's Eve.
Gerri, my Northeast Elementary classmate,
friend, and sixth-grade steady for a week,
sat in the row ahead, straight blonde hair straggling
down in blue light while my hands found warmth
and, yes, lots more beneath the knitted poncho
Mimi and I had pulled up to our chins.
Even back then, it seemed a stretch, at best,
to call this journey "educational" —
though, true, the movie had come from a book,
Paul Gallico's potboiler that no doubt
had passed, well-thumbed, across the teachers' lounge.
Gerri was flanked by Eleonora and Sandra
in the row's dim brine, face tilted up,
my good pal's pretty profile pale before
the tidal wave's inexorable blow
that, literally, turned the world upside-down.

How long had it been since Julie, emissary
urged on by their clique, had crossed the schoolyard,
said that Gerri "liked" me, and commenced

the brief life cycle of our sixth-grade fling?
How long since I'd joined Gerri on her block —
finally alone, the two of us on swings,
both waiting, kicking dirt half-heartedly,
talking of who would call the other next,
too young, just then, to take the plunge and kiss?
Only thirteen, already I was lamenting
opportunities missed, while Mimi squirmed —
fifteen, an older woman, mouse-brown hair
framing her round face — offering sure access
hidden from view, the Purser's cry that "Climbing
to another deck will kill you all!"
echoing through the darkness, actors quaking
at the choice to stay put or ascend.

It's true that Young Love loves an audience
as much as sampling pleasures still taboo….
The Christmas tree, propped up to form a ladder,
offered Life, or so Gene Hackman fumed —
playing the sideburned Preacher, flushed and sweating,
suddenly gentler when he counseled Susan,
(young, not-quite-love interest), "You can't climb
in that long gown, it'll just have to come off."
Come off indeed…. Gerri glanced back once
or twice, shot me a smile at some point,
our near-front row in plain sight of our teachers
if they looked or cared, beams shooting through
dim light, unbraiding overhead as if
in counterpoint to what took place on screen.

Months later, Mimi and I, virgins no more,
would ride the summer swelter on the swells
of sex, infatuation, and release

denied as often as will power allowed.
She wrote poems, listened to the Osmond brothers,
Mormons in matching white suits whom I mocked,
and, one day, on our way back home from Grant's
(where else could young teens go?), we rested on
the concrete platform of a curbside drain.
Trees — thick-leafed, edged with sunlight — lined the street,
and soon, from nowhere, Gerri and her sister
rose before us, braking. Radiant
upon her bike, she, too, was heading toward
the five-and-ten we'd just left, killing time
as August ebbed, elated to meet by chance,
our small talk so at ease, our close connection
suddenly so palpable to all,
that Mimi blanched. They biked off. We walked home.

It's strange how love dies — silently, at first;
through flooded stairwells and companionways,
we swim, lungs bursting, hoping we'll emerge
where we belong, unsure of where that is.
Mimi and I broke up; ninth grade began,
my ex exiled to high school, but I found
Gerri had cooled, transformed in those few weeks,
into a stranger whose own ex, she laughed,
had been "a twat." I flinched. She'd ditched her old
friends Eleonora and Sandra, flunked assignments,
smoked in the girls' bathroom, vices all
that made her seem more sexy, dangerous,
and guess what happened when I asked her out?
Still, Gerri was kind, saying — I think sincerely —
she hoped I hadn't broken up with Mimi
because of her. I winced and said I hadn't —
not the first lie that I'd ever told,

but one that stung.... The Preacher's fall toward fire —
the knowledge that, of all fates, this was his —
had galled him as much as the blaze itself,
having swung to the valve beyond the gangway
where, hand over hand, he'd turned the wheel
from which he hung, released the burning steam
that threatened those he led, then lost his grip.
I felt that, too, except without the scalding,
all-consuming pain, and instant death.

So this was growing up: I'd crushed someone
who'd given herself to me "body and soul,"
as she'd have said back then, and did, in tears,
only to stand by helplessly and watch
another I loved, or liked, or lusted for,
sink in the flood that rose around us all.
The next year, Gerri's family moved away
to Massachusetts: one day she was there,
among us, in the halls, in faded jeans,
and gone the next, her name in purple typeface
smelling sickly sweet upon the ditto
listing absent students. By week's end,
even her name was gone. I hope, somewhere,
she found her morning after, as Carol Lynley,
lip synching Maureen McGovern's hit
before disaster struck, herself found love,
the ocean's vista writhing furiously
in Panavision, as she found the light.

But, really, who knows what takes place beyond
the final reel, bright white lights coming on
to blind us once the credits have run out,
poncho smoothed down, hair rearranged, the faces

that we wear prepared for scrutiny
by lovers, friends, and strangers; stand-ins, stuntmen
tumbling everywhere in memory,
however grown up we believe we are —
Gerri and Mimi watchful in the dark,
like those who fought for Life, who like me hoped
and feared they'd one day get what they deserved,
but pressed on anyway, despite the script
that wrote their fates for them, deprived all choice,
flood rising close behind them as they'd climbed
up to the bottom, lost in paradox,
preserved or punished, hoping to be saved.

A Nonsense Name

Saturday + Sapphire; Brentwood, L.I., NY

The near-drowned crow I found one Saturday,
with deep blue, jewel-like eyes — "sapphires," I said —
could have but one name: Satire. Stunned, not dead,
he'd drifted toward the filter with debris,
dead bugs, and now, rag-wrapped, dwelled in a box,
one hour removed from his recovery.
My dad had fished him out. "He looks okay,"
my mother ventured.
                                        Eyes expressionless,
Satire, black feathers slicked down, shook off flecks
of water, glanced up toward the sky, toward us,
head tilted slightly — as if, shocked awake,
he now remembered where he'd meant to go
unnamed, unmoved, in enigmatic black,
beyond this rescue and our patio.

Aerial Views of Levittown

This aerial snapshot holds potato fields,
tree-clumps, a few dirt roads, the Hempstead Plains
that Dutch and German immigrants had bullied
into farmland, ground that bore Long Island's
celebrated tubers — wrinkled, eyed —
peeking from bushel bags on market floors.
The War was over, and the Bomb had won.
Grumman Aircraft, thriving in Bethpage,
had groomed twelve thousand Hellcats for the hell
they'd give in the Pacific while, at home,
farsighted William Levitt saw the future
in those wasted acres. Soon, the flood
of soldiers and their brides would settle down
in Cape Cod homes he'd coax up from the earth
a world away from New York City's boroughs,
Dresden's ruins, the shores of Normandy.

The second view confirms his prophecy
with curvilinear streets and cul-de-sacs
served by the parkways Robert Moses carved
across two counties to the wilderness
of Wantagh and Great River, roads that trapped
tired parents in traffic jams, their kids asleep,
sand-blasted after Jones Beach, homeward bound.
A hundred new homes went up every week
for families not shut out by faith or race,
T.V. antennas capturing a world
blue-gray and blinding, roiled and Romper Roomed,

its eye turned on us as we turned from it
— and Levitt, former Seabee, gave thanksgiving
for the golden nematode that chewed
through fields that farmers, eager to unload
their headaches, sold dirt-cheap without regrets.

So Levittown — America — was born.
Long Island's coastline glittered north to south,
idyllic vistas dazzling from afar —
and summer smelled like pools and barbecue.
There, for a while at least, the crop survived,
for sale in bags that bulged red, white, and blue —
gray-brown potatoes pressed to string-mesh windows,
pleading that someone bring them to a boil.

Triolet in Violet

The twilight sky looks purple, like merlot.
Where morning glories climb, mouths closed at sunset,
words spent, we sip quietly. I know
the twilight, liminal, like good merlot,
leaves us uncertain: should we stay or go?
There's light, but how much darker will it get,
now that the sky's gone purple? — while, below,
dark flowers multiply with every sunset.

For My Step-Daughter, Who Missed the Apparition

For Catherine, in her father's custody for the summer, and for Jane, Rodgers Forge, Maryland, 2008

In our small parcel of suburbia,
my neighbors straggle outside after rain,
drawn by the sight: bright band, celestial arc

blending to indigo. Weightless, unreal,
it rose in silence when our backs were turned
this afternoon in spring, its end unknown,

its origin light rays at altitudes
beyond our reach, prismatic, luminous.
Hungry for spectacle, I join my wife —

sun showers, in short bursts, fall. The kids run riot
on rain-drenched lawns. A neighbor brings his camera.
Spider-Man — mask off, in ill-matched sneakers

and sports goggles with corrective lenses —
peers up when his mom says, "Watch the sky."
Each parent understands this moment calls

for awe — that awe is possible, today,
and should be shared, or taught — though novelty
compels us, too: we're human, after all.

Is this the same arc, bow without an arrow,
Noah showed to Japheth, Shem, and Ham
after the Flood, God's sign of covenant

that, next time, he'd select a different method
to destroy the world? I'll bet they smirked,
Well, that's *a comfort* — though I wonder if

what's more important is that they remembered
something — fiction, mystery, or myth —
that joined them to the world, the world to them.

The storm's still moving west — a few stray drops
now spattering on impact — to abandon,
spectral in its wake, a ghostly version

of the crescent near its counterpart —
now there are two, though one's translucent, pale.
A boy who wears, festooned with flying saucers,

pajamas with feet that tread on grass and sidewalk,
yells, "Hey, Dad," and everyone looks up —
my wife, too — at the double vision floating

strangely overhead. Did Noah's story
help sons grasp the image and hold on?
The mind is restless, though: *Focus, look up*

goes only so far with our kids, ourselves,
before we look away, distracted, bored,
or, simply, elsewhere, carried off by time

into a different moment, memory
impatient for dominion. By the time
I stand beside my wife, mothers conversing,

step-daughter out of town, wondering if
she's yet been introduced to Roy G Biv
in science class, refraction's miracle,

they're gone, both arcs sent to oblivion.
Conditions changed; they simply don't exist,
while here on earth, kids quarrel, shriek at freeze tag,

happily indifferent to the loss.
Show's over; dinnertime. Our small talk dies,
the neighbors hail farewell and wander in,

shepherding offspring cranky at the change,
hungry or nap-deprived. Each loss is different;
so, too, every gain: we have a story,

now, my wife and I, our hopes invoked
with every telling — lasting, clarified —
its sole flaw — that it must be told at all —

its gift as well:
Catherine, had you been home,
by happy accident, the storm delayed,
you might have been the first to go outside.

Blue Panther

Fancier than the fanciest Gloucester Fancy,
canaries not of a feather flocked, flashed past,
and, parrot-sized, kept changing as they flew,
caged multicolored singing specimens
jailed under bars so widely spaced apart
each fluttered through and fled away to danger,
beauty beyond control, ill-suited cage
vanishing as they left. I was so angry
I might have woken then … But one remained,
more Rilkean than avian, transformed —
blue panther padding toward me, whiskered muzzle
turned up, eyes aglint in recognition,
as if fixed to choose, above all others,
one who'd known him in some other guise.

A Parable of Flight

Wouldn't it be great if lizards flew,
the world's mind thought and, thinking, made it true.
The pterosaur, ascendant in the sky,
would last an age and, over eons, die.

The world's mind thought and, thinking, made it true.
From trilobite to slow triceratops,
some good ideas would, over eons, die.
The bird-hipped dinosaur took baby steps

past trilobite, beyond triceratops,
till archaeopteryx, the feathered lizard,
sought the sky. No time for baby steps —
sharp claws and teeth protected it from hazard,

though the creature looked less bird than lizard.
Was its blood, perhaps, already warm?
Sharp claws and teeth protected it from hazard
when it fought, inflicting real harm —

the blood of carrion is always warm.
Who flew beside the starling and the crow?
The passenger pigeon, though it meant no harm,
rose up in great flocks shadowing the snow,

but who survived? The starling and the crow.
And yet, the world's mind also loves a joke —
ostrich and emu, striding over snow,
lush veldt, or outback took another look

(because the world's mind always loves a joke),
and said, *No, thanks*. The concept in reverse.
The dodo, too, from which a single look,
sad-eyed, brought traders' clubs down with a curse,

followed survival's trend-line in reverse.
Would it have fared much better in the sky?
It couldn't tell a blessing from a curse....
Earth-bound unfortunate, it never flew.

Snow in Baghdad

January 11, 2008

The snow so rare that people call it "rain,"
wet flakes touch earth and pavement, ruins and wreckage,
the muezzins' call to prayer, the morning's music,
calmer, quieter. Five years of war,
and, now, this peace: unasked for, temporary,
Americans in desert camouflage
stationed conspicuously, brushing snow
from shoulders, guns, while snowball fights ensue
among the young: the sound of Arabic,
English in softer tones, spatter of white
on impact, laughter as the traffic slows,
checkpoints and concrete walls disguised, erased,
and one old resident exclaims in wonder,
"In all my life I've never seen such rain."

2.

It seems, just now,
To be happening so very fast…
— Philip Larkin

Rondel for a Timepiece Not Yet Obsolete

In an age awash with digital devices...plugged-in people of all ages are opting to leave their old timepiece at home.

Analog watch — wrist-worn circle of time,
ticking the days away in symmetries
Swiss-made and sleepless, tireless mysteries
concealed by stainless steel — your hours rhyme

in sets of twelve. Essential in your prime,
object of habit now, set me at ease,
analog wristwatch, worn circle of time.
Keep ticking away the days in symmetries

that call to mind the past: sleek hands that climb,
pointing across a face that's not a face,
as if in search of lost simplicities....
Earth's orbit round the sun your paradigm,
how soon will you run down, worn-out?...Circle of time.

For Jacob Kurtzberg

Better known as Jack Kirby (1917-1993)

Nothing beyond his power, in Mineola,
drawing furiously, the artist Jacob,
"Jack" to friends and fans, finds one idea
compels him, hurtling, through every job —

for money, sure, but also (lit cigar stub
trailing smoke) for love: he knows his genre
offers myth, and heroes need a problem
that will test their powers. In Mineola,

working from home (postwar suburbia),
an East Side kid, Jack punched his way past trouble,
gave the world Captain America,
and more: the pantheon of heroes Jacob

draws for Marvel now. Aye, there's the rub
(eraser-shreds brushed back, tabula rasa
of the next page waiting): credit-grabbing
wordsmith Stan will think this new idea

is his alone; still, pages fill the sofa,
ready for the shoot. No time for "grub" —
Jack's on a mission, as at Omaha
ten days after the landing, when the job

eclipsed, by far, some petty contract's quota.
But what foe must his quartet face and clobber?
— *a silver angel falls, his gleaming aura*
crackling as he wakes in fiery rubble,
nothing beyond his power.

A Dog and a Wolf

John Wolf, a 7-year-old son of a butcher…wandered away yesterday afternoon from his father's shop, and could not find his way back. He was accompanied by a large yellow dog….
— New York Times, *December 10, 1879*

In Lower Manhattan — seven years old, lost —
John Wolf, a butcher's son, finds he's followed
by the dog that acts as his familiar,
guardian mongrel loyal to the core,
barking at passers by who pose no danger,
growling at those who only want to help.

They shrink back as he snarls, azure-eyed
and yellow-furred, along the Bowery's cobbles,
till one policeman braves the canine's valor,
taking the boy's hand gently in his own,
asking his full name, where he's wandered from.
The dog, eyes watchful, follows past the squalor,

trash, and tenements, back to headquarters
where a Matron Webb accepts the child
into her charge, one of the street's lost urchins
(every day brings more: the poor, the homeless,
pushed from their doors to work, neglected lives
that neither prayer nor poverty redeems),

but must the dog accompany him, too?
He won't step down as sentry, meets her gaze
and stares her down, this animal, this cur,
unblinking, whiskered, while the lost kids laugh —
the cop, too. Why's that animal still here?
Is this his final stand or last resort

before he's dragged away? Will John Wolf cry
at losing his protector, or rush up
and throw his arms around good Matron Webb?
She'll never know: the elder Wolf's arrived,
his butcher's smock still smeared, eyes frantic still
to the delight of young Wolf, dog, and cop.

But Matron Webb feels ill-used, sorely troubled;
however many lost she gathers up,
the streets keep more and lend them only briefly
to her care. What life will young Wolf have —
what life did she have caring for the brothers
lost so long ago she can't remember?

Growling at those who only want to help,
the dog, eyes watchful, follows past the squalor
that neither prayer nor poverty redeems,
as if this final stand, this last resort
would bring delight to father and young Wolf
lost, once, so long ago he can't remember.

Times Square Post Cards

1. The Great White Way, 1910s

A full moon shines above the Great White Way —
the Astor, Strand, and Palace Theatres,
signs stemmed and serifed in electric lights
against the sky, some lettered vertically

as if to lure the gaze of passers-by
downward to doors that open on the square
to billiards, burlesque, café, theater —
the din of music, dancing, dinnertime.

Who goes there? Everyone, where once the broad
lane of the Wappingers became the way
the Dutch pushed northward from New Amsterdam;

where, later, Forty-Second Street and Seventh
Avenue converged at what was called
Longacre Square before the *New York Times*

moved uptown and, on New Year's Eve, drew crowds
with fireworks sent bursting overhead,
first trial of long tradition. Is the moon

in this old post card still the brightest light?
Nobody looks above the Square at night.

2. New *Times* Building, 1900s

The year was 1904. Newspaper Row
was old news. Adolph Ochs had closed up shop
and moved his business to the subway stop
that bears his paper's name, as would the Square

by April of that year. If fireworks-flame
was dangerous, descending from the sky
to burn on cobbles, sidestepped by the mob
each New Year's Eve, a lighted ball would do,

and has done, now, for past a century.
Based on a photograph (to judge by placement
of pedestrians who cross through snow),

one post card shows a black man derbied, garbed
in boots, gold-buttoned greatcoat, reins in hand,
carriage and horse beside, awaiting hire —

one more New Yorker in a time of change.
Behind him, built to fit its tapered lot,
twenty-five stories that defined the *Times*

reach toward a winter sky icy but clear
as if to tell the world, "The future's here."

3. Astor's Knickerbocker, 1906-1921

Six Times Square, Astor's Knickerbocker, rose
proudly above the streets, its mansard roof
and brickwork proof of luxury within
where Maxfield Parrish painted thirty feet

of *Old King Cole* before the hotel closed
in 1921. That very year,
Caruso, longtime resident, took on
a new engagement where, beyond our realm,

one hopes that he's still singing. Once, he gave
his shoes to some poor soul trapped on a breadline
outside the hotel, once sang the anthems

of three nations from a balcony
to mark the Armistice. Astor himself
had passed from earthly life in 1912

when, from an ocean liner sprayed with ice,
he might have seen the Northern Lights aflame
above the crown jewel of the White Star line

before it sank. What else would he have seen?
White light, the Knickerbocker's bar agleam.

4. Broadway Buskers, 1920s; Billboards, 2000s

The Great White Way's performers, black and white,
cast members cast out, gathered on the "beach,"
triangle of concrete in Times Square's midst,
angling for applause. From underground,

the subway rumbled grates and spoiled songs
already drowned by horns, policeman's whistles,
trollies, white-tired Caddies rattling by
throughout the Twenties. Some — the lucky few —

escaped to great acclaim, others slunk back
to claim the very place they'd once surrendered
at this crossroads. Remember Cohan's song,

"Tell all the gang at Forty-Second Street"?
That gang was out of work, busking for food,
an agent's nod.
                              Today, the *Times* headquarters

that loomed over them is tenantless,
kept up to serve the global aims of Coke,
Samsung, Prudential as mere billboard space,

its long-concealed terra-cotta surface
vanished like the stars of vaudeville.

5. A Crystal Ball, 1907-2000s (1943, 1944)

The countdown from the *Times* roof still goes on,
the incandescent crystal moon or sun,
lit from within, descending. We look on,
awaiting verdict on the very second

that the New Year strikes: a sudden flash,
time's speed made real. One year, a century,
and everyone's transformed: top hats, sleek furs
give way to plain fedoras, knitted scarves,

new slang, the latest fads that take a place
among our gains and losses every year.
The young midshipmen who sought out Times Square

for cheap laughs or a night's companionship;
the G.I.s who returned on leave from Europe,
briefly, to the boroughs; WACs and WAVEs —

they, too, met in the Square, though wartime blackouts
called for more restraint: a minute's silence
for the brave who'd sacrificed their lives,

until recorded bells rang in the year
for all who kept their faith, heads bowed in prayer.

6. The Bond's Clothing Store "Spectacular Waterfall Sign," 1948-1954

The statues locked above the Bond's montage,
by day, looked nude: grim, neo-classical,
one man and (it's presumed) his mate stood watch,
divided by a disc that told the time

in context of the sum of customers
who bought Bond's every hour. Men bought "clothes,"
women "apparel," but neither fit these giants
who, at dusk, revealed themselves as dressed

in strands of lights switched on. Six years they stood,
titanic, tantalizing, finally toppled
from their place by Pepsi. Douglas Leigh

designed them and the sign that brought them down —
betrayed by their creator! And the falls
that rushed, suspended in the space between,

store-length, powered by twenty-three huge pumps,
ran dry as well.
                Colossi, did you hear
the crowds who snickered daily as they passed

below you, the deluge that sprayed its mist?
Briefly, Times Square and you could co-exist.

The Ghosts at Ground Zero

I leapt — I shouldn't say "into the void"
but into blinding sunlight — from the fire
that burst through doors and roared past, from the smoke
that poured its trail, black ash, and boiling heat
through restaurants, kitchens, halls, and offices.
Given the choice, would you have burned to death,
waiting for rescue while walls and girders shuddered,
the power drained from monitors gone dark,
or would you, too, have jumped toward clear, bright sunlight
into a pristine moment when, resigned,
you rose up, weightless, till the fall took hold?
Not every ghost had time to ask that question.
The lucky ones weren't those who answered it.
But what's left now? A hole in memory
we should have occupied with real lives
and lapses, not the perfect selves that grief
has made from us, like airbrushed photographs
tacked up to help identify the missing,
though they look like no one ever found.
It's strange to think of all the time I used
up calculating fallout risks and futures
for a future crushed: we'd reached the edge
of some new precipice but looked ahead
instead of down, where steel and concrete rumbled,
or above, where gleaming metal neared —
behind us all, the force of history
and rage so deep it, too, was bottomless.
Now we are one (except to those who knew us),

a scroll of names, an honor roll called out
in yearly rituals, commemorations
in search of meaning or, at least, an end.
Except there's no end. It goes on and on.
New buildings rise on old ground, new foundations
laid to serve another skyward surge
toward sun and stars that holds a double purpose:
to memorialize your ghosts reduced to dust
and, finally, help you to forget us, too
— as if a shining spire could do that now
when we know what it rose from far below.
I've got the time — all time — to watch what plays
out in our names, to contemplate our ties
to all and to each other, to the ground
we walked on every day, sealed under asphalt,
traffic and crowds we left when we rode up
a hundred stories closer to the sky —
This ground that's ours, this ground we didn't want
where history stakes its place and claims our lives.
My last call, dialed from work, went straight to phone mail,
where I spoke the same words others did —
sorry and *love you all* through screams and static,
noise and sirens. What else could I say,
cracked windows falling forward, sheets of glass
struck by debris before they left the frame?
I only wish I that I could call right now
and this time reach you with a message from
the ghosts at Ground Zero trapped here for all time —
trailing like smoke through walls and waterfalls,
while the world, relentlessly on course
hurls you toward something worse, or back to us —
to say, before we fade from memory,

We remember all, and we remember nothing,
not even our faces, immortal, vaporized,
lost to the abyss in light that falls between
what had to happen and what never could.

Suicide of an Old Man

New York Times, *December 7, 1879*

The facts are few. It happened in Elmira.
The *laborer, well-to-do* — an immigrant,
or not, we'll never know — was touched by fire,
a *fit* (what else to call it?), that turned saint,
sinner, or soul between, David Fitzgerald
toward his end. What *labor* had been his?
What symptoms or behavior had been herald?
To what force did he finally answer, "Yes,"
seeking the means — smashed bottle, carving knife,
straight razor freshly rinsed — to *cut his throat*
to-night from ear to ear, taking the life
he must have valued once? (Or maybe not.)
Insanity's no answer, though the text he
features in records his age: *Near sixty*.

Return from Slumberland

After Winsor McKay's Little Nemo In Slumberland
Sunday comics page, New Year's holiday, 1905

When Nemo bends to touch the number 9
offered by Father Time (in Slumberland
all things are possible), he feels just fine,
glad to have grown so fast. Where will it end?
Holding a single digit in each hand,
he's 15 — no, he's older every time
that Time bestows new numbers in a dream

too colorful to doubt. 4 paired with 8 —
"Enough!" he shouts, at heart a small boy still,
fat, balding in the mirror Time has brought
close to astonished eyes. Oh, this is cruel,
take back the numbers! Soon, Nemo is well,
the child we know and love. But winged Time leaves,
called elsewhere on some errand, what he gives

sought for across the globe yet always less
than he withholds.... Alone, the boy selects
a 99 (as always, curious)
from Time's store of millennia, effects
concealed, the change that no one quite expects
beyond a six-year-old's imagination:
This is who he'll *be*. Where's everyone?

Where's Father Time, the way home? Bent, near blind,
an old man, Nemo once, turns from a sky
sunless, star-crowded, wondering who'll find
him in this cold, his world and century
changed, too: some barren moonscape....
And he'll cry,
"Am I an old man, Mama?" when he wakes —
startled, restored — however long it takes.

3.

The hunt sweeps out upon the plain
And the garden darkens.
— Louise Bogan

Dark Horse

This moonlit night we've come upon a horse —
his equine profile looms above barbed wire,
so close we might have touched him accidentally
as we pass along this country road
on foot, our flashlights small moons flicking off.
We don't want to startle him: he's still,
and we can't see his eyes — is he asleep,
awake and watching us, or in the grip
of dread? He might be dangerous at night.
By day, he's chestnut-brown, but now, he's shadow,
eyes invisible, mane moonlight-tinged,
the hills behind him dim, vertiginous
with all the history his kind have known
entwined with ours, each day and every darkness.

Black Cat and Rescued Tom

A black cat, velvet-smooth, splays out on wood,
possessing the piano. In New York,
a tom, tuxedo-furred, rests lion-paws

against a wine-glass base. It's his, he thinks,
like everything. The two once shared a home
when we were married; they no longer do.

The black cat yawns, awakes to arch her back,
sharp silhouette that heightens and contracts
to face the futon-beam. The New York tom,

Baltimore-born, was rescued from its streets.
We had to rescue him, given his state —
war-torn and ailing, blood caked at the eyes

he'd scratched compulsively, who knows how long.
The velvet girl sits tall, studies my lap's
terrain, its tempting denim. In New York,

the tom bounds clumsily toward friend or stranger,
equal citizens approved for passage
in his kingdom. Here, wary of dangers

that do not exist, Black Velvet tests
the distance to my knee. The tom's afraid
of pitchers — someone must have emptied one

upon him in his months without a home —
but, no, he can't recall the other cat,
or mornings when we caught him in a towel —

I pried his jaw; you aimed the pill syringe;
he kicked but never even tried to scratch.
Even then, he offered with his gaze

a look that I'd call *human*, though it wasn't,
kind, though kindness lay beyond his ken.
As if she's never made this move before,

the black cat cries, climbs down and clamps herself,
claws out, against my leg. The tom — tuxedoed,
calm — rolls over on his back and purrs,

cured now, above the fray, his belly white —
semi-retired, as all toms should be,
fur luminous in darkness, lion rumbling

on a quilt hand-crafted by your aunt —
a wedding gift I slept beneath with you,
both cats close by, though I no longer do.

The Ex-Friends

The ex-friends like you still, but they're wary,
when chance meetings force them to extend
the courtesy they'd once have given freely.

At first, you thought their distance temporary —
time away to find themselves, or mend.
The ex-friends like you still, but they're weary,

faced with deadlines, obligations daily
undertaken, though they still intend,
they say, with courtesy once given freely,

to call you back, though it's unnecessary —
painful, even — since you "understand":
the ex-friends you still like are feeling wary,

wondering if they've fooled you — fooled you *really*?
So much work is needed to pretend
the courtesy they'd once have given freely,

so you part ways, thoughtful, solitary —
what thoughtless word, long past, had marked the end?
The ex-friends, like you, still are feeling wary
but relieved...They smiled. You set them free.

Letter to a New Arrival

> *Attn: African-American family. This is coming from Lindenhurst community. Lindenhurst is 84% white population. You don't belong here!!! Please leave Lindenhurst as soon as you can. It will be better for all of us. Find a town where there are more people like you. Sorry if this is rude, but it's the truth.*
>
> — Anonymous letter to Lindenhurst, L.I. family, postmarked May 19, 2015

This salutation isn't meant to soothe,
so don't say *dear. Attention* gets it right.
Sorry if this is rude, but it's the truth:

Tone matters in thank-you notes and racist threats.
Claim that you speak for everyone who's white,
but show some class and lose the epithets,

or else the family you'd run out of town
might get so mad, they stand their ground and fight.
Say they'd be *better off among their own*

as if, in some strange way, you want to help.
Throw in a *please*. It's good to be polite.
But don't obscure the meaning if you hope

to wake one morning to a moving van,
or to a home abandoned overnight,
shades drawn down. *Find a new town when you can*

shows admirable restraint when we recall
what sundown towns once promised. In the light
of morning, mail the printout. All is well —

you'll have your neighbors' lasting gratitude
in coded words and whispers, "You did right."
You wrote the note they didn't have to write —

and the truth is, you won't stop at being rude.

Breakthrough

Just a year ago, neuroscientists couldn't do much better
than distinguish thoughts of faces from thoughts of places....
No longer.... Now research has broken the 'content' barrier.

The word "eureka" triggers, in the brain,
a pattern neuro-imagers can read,
though, at the present time, ideas and language

still remain a challenge. Better by far
is our ability to map intent —
not what you do, but what you plan to do —

as when a subject, told to think "subtraction,"
demonstrates in his prefrontal scan
the very patterns we record as well

in subjects solving problems at a desk.
From math to murder, traffic lights to love,
each thought provokes a corresponding image

we can track and measure in the cortex
accurately, when the data's in.
Soon, perhaps, our means — this clumsy headgear —

will give way to more efficient methods:
headbands sensor-ringed, remote controlled
and microchipped, that gather, from far off,

our passing whims and ordinary days.
Think of it: every time the human mind,
vast storehouse of our lives and all we've seen,

responds to stimuli, what it discloses
adds more to our growing database
of patterns, paradigms.
                                        What we will do

with this new window on the mind's evasions,
hopes, and inmost secrets; on misdeeds
conceived or carried out, resentments hidden,

we'll consider at another time.

The Woods

Brentwood, L.I., ca. late '60s and beyond; for Gary

The woods closed in — who knew how long they grew,
planted or wild, around your rented house,
the short cut to your back door beaten down
past stunted pines, the outhouse that survived,
weed-choked and long disused, shedding its paint
like flakes of lead-filled snow against the ground.
This was suburbia, your house a remnant
of the rural past, your unpaved driveway
haven to your mother's humble Rambler
parked, metallic green, outside the locked
garage that held your landlord's secret trove.
The house, re-shingled gray box, occupied
more land than it required, a full-sized acre
that took in the woods, low brush, grape arbor
draped on trees, untrellised, overgrown.
The yard was weeds: crabgrass and onion grass
I pulled up for the smell, translucent bulb
off-white and layered, though nothing at the core
seemed worth the trouble of unpeeling it.
More worthy were the woods: blackberry bushes —
jumbled, thorn-spiked — furled through uncut grass,
fern-stalks that grew straight up, the berries — green,
reddish, black-purple finally — luminous.
We got some; birds got more. And in the fall,
I looked for goldenrod, sun-yellow rows
that split green stems: disliked, but everywhere,
while dead leaves crunched like gift-wrap underfoot.

❧

Some summer days, I'd play entrepreneur,
unfold a table on a verge of crabgrass
near the woods, the intersection dead,
ready to sell whatever left me bored,
price scrawled on paper signs in ballpoint pen:
comics at half price (6¢ in the '60s),
monsters who'd tumbled down the metal chutes
of gum machines, enclosed in plastic bubbles;
Major Matt Mason, whose inner wire had snapped,
the spaceman's leg impossible to pose.
Above me, cooing loudly, pigeons gathered,
fugitives from the coop in Doreen's yard
(tar paper roof nailed carelessly in place)
— Doreen, the older woman, ten years old,
who'd let me touch the soft down on their backs
once, in the dim light, trilling in their berths.
They'd cram the phone lines, iridescent necks
bobbing to match their aimless wandering
while I sat with the junk I sold for coins
or lost to what was called "five-finger discount"
in those days, and now, for all I know.
Enrico and Alex were Sicilian thieves,
brothers to fear, you said, keeping your distance
while I ran my stand, my own last name
southern Italian, too. Your name was German,
each of us subject to some vice or flaw
assigned by race, faith, or ethnicity,
but in ourselves conveniently ignored —
the era's birthright handed down to us.
I folded up the table, brought the toys,

unwanted misfits, home, then sought the shade
we found together, kicking through the woods
where crickets, gold-winged, burrowed under bricks.

❧

What did your landlord keep inside the room
that led to the garage? You told me once.
A heavy wardrobe stood before the door.
Your father, rage-choked when he wasn't sleeping,
bent on knowing what his rent paid for
(and whether it was something he could use),
summoned your brother Johnny, not yet drafted,
to his side. Together, they could move
what one could not. Your mother looked on, too,
black beehive sprayed to beauty school perfection
while the massive wardrobe scraped gray paint
right off the mud room floor. But what they found
repelled your father, given all he'd spent —
not just in curiosity and sweat,
but hopes he'd raised only to be rewarded
with — what else but trash? Impressed, you told
me of old-fashioned dresses mothballed, hung
in neat rows; ladies' hats, adorned with feathers,
shoes strewn in profusion, stacked in boxes
squashed or scattered, brand names long defunct
(whose thrill was this — your mother's or your own?)
the path to the garage impassable
before your dad, disgusted, slammed the door.
This anteroom — did you discover there
the mink-pelts that we played with, beads for eyes,
their bottom jaws black clamps that snapped securely

to high-fashion collars of the past?
(The clamps beneath their snouts opened and closed
in synch to speech we voiced on their behalf.)
But there was more: a slice of wedding cake,
yellowed, you claimed, rose-trimmed beneath smeared glass
dust-steeped, uninterrupted in repose
for decades, light-starved, saved for someone dead.

❧

Your landlord — was she born in Italy
or New York City? — moved out, rumor said,
even before the neighborhood went up
around her property. Widowed, divorced,
she'd fled back to her native borough, Brooklyn,
withered and grown rich. The cake was hers,
preserved because her husband, killed in war,
had died before their anniversary
— or had he casually deserted her?
The truth was anybody's guess, and ours.
Perhaps those arbor-vines had once provided
grapes for home-made wine: black-purple, bitter,
thick with sediment. One day, I looked
down, saw the sharp edge of a buried relic
in the dirt: a whelk-shell, perforated —
"No, it couldn't be," your father scoffed,
"maybe a broken cup." But there it was:
the very shell that held a snail's flesh,
scungilli, scraped clean, after some lost feast,
the family joined on benches, tables hazed
in steam and stogie-smoke, wine gurgling freely
from ceramic jugs, while laughter struck

among dead strangers we would never know.
I picked the dirt off, brought the shell to light.
What was the great indignity your father
took to heart, killed six-packs to forget
or stew upon, slouched on a frayed chaise lounge?
To him, you were no ordinary son —
not when, on Halloween, adorned in drag,
you swayed, bewigged, at ease in your new guise,
cheeks rouged, mouth lipsticked by your mother's hand.
Why did you ride your grown half-sister's bike,
its downswept bar the certain giveaway,
and not your own? While Johnny sneered, your father
called you "sissy." How it must have hurt.
Even today, I see him parked beside
the arbor, dressed in black pants, sleeveless T-shirt,
glowering at us both, the heat oppressive
some mid-summer weekend afternoon.

One day, I met your brother's hippie girlfriend,
midriff bared, disheveled honey-hair
swaying across her shoulders, hips in jeans
as, giggling, she stepped from the used Corvette
whose engine Johnny gunned at night for laughs.
We stood together, you and I, bewildered
by this creature: I admired her body,
you, her clothes, your father snarling curtly
on the driveway dirt, mother aghast
at this new adversary. But the worst
was yet to come: your brother and the same
girl rumbling up the drive another day,

the car doors slamming to the news they'd wed:
Johnny, in green dress Army uniform,
the bride in white veil, wedding mini-dress,
and blue eye shadow, laughing as if stoned —
probably just champagne. We stayed away
and went on with whatever else we did
that sent each day to the oblivion
that held the rest. Johnny, I later heard,
had found himself dispatched to Vietnam,
but made it back — on furlough or for good? —
home to his hippie bride. Our friendship stalled
before sixth grade: we didn't say a word
for years, shared not one class. You grew up gawky,
sullen, pigeon-toed, and acne-plagued
but, worse for you, too feminine in clothes
your mother snatched up at John's Bargain Store —
outmoded shirts and polyester slacks
remaindered out of season, sold in bins.
You graduated early but endured
(rumor again) long screaming fights and years
of beatings till your father threw you out.
The world was not a place that offered shelter
to men like yourself. Where could you go?
One day, a last blow sent you out at last,
clothes stuffed inside a duffel bag, the shapes
of trees unnerving as you stormed outside
alone, or met a friend and drove away,
your mother's shadow passing at the window
nervously, the locked garage still locked.

❧

What did the world once hold, sap trickling down
gashed pine-trunks to the needle-bed beneath,
tar honey-gold, then black on bark stained white?
Broad-leafed, the grapevines clung and intertwined
along a brace of pine trees, rose to clasp
an oak's low-hanging branches, bell-shaped curtain
clustered with fruit not ripe enough to taste,
though, yes, we tasted it. And it was sour,
green grapes, green like the predator I glimpsed,
at waist-height, past the arbor, balancing
in quiet meditation, on a branch.
You might have gone inside, or I was out
exploring on my own the woods we shared,
amazed a picture from my *Golden Guide*
had sprung to life, its jagged forelegs raised
as if in prayer, leaf-green, waiting with patience
for the next unfortunate who'd pass,
tiny or blind enough to catch and eat.
Who'd share this miracle? I whirled and ran
to your back door, rapped on the frame, called out,
then rushed back to discover it was gone —
a praying mantis waiting for its prey
so strange and still it hadn't seemed quite real.
Birds called; the bracket fungus formed its shelves,
fan-like, on rotten logs that sank in mulch.
Beached among shards of glass, smashed bottles caught
the sun beside the rock that shattered them,
sea-green and sticky. Everyone was gone
but me, and nothing moved — but that's not true,
in woods, in summer, something always moves,

shudders or flies away. The woods encroached
on three sides of your house (not that the house)
was ever yours) and must be gone by now,
erased as you, your family, all of us
who bear our memories and mysteries
throughout our lives, will make our own departures,
bound or solitary, in due course.

Ante Meridiem

A child's vocation

This coffee can will shelter them in tin —
beads speed across bright metal. Punched with holes,
a snap-on lid. Today, 7 a.m.,
I'll hunt and gather, wet grass placed within
as if to hoodwink compound eyes. Who rules
the sunlit, shadowed underbrush? It's *them* —

instinct machines who leap, against the odds,
from sneaker-soles or rivals' mandibles,
to lair or leaf. *Ante meridiem,*
what's death? I guess, to fleeing arthropods,
I am.

Dead Man Walking

John 11:1-12:50

At first he was a sideshow: the dead man raised,
someone to gawk at during his three squares
or trips back from the privy: *he's alive,*
all right — reason to think about those rumors
and strange sayings making all the rounds
before you draw conclusions that they're bunk.
But, later, it was strange: back from the dead,
whatever chamber held him, he seemed lost —
as if the Man from Nazareth and he
had shared some secret no one should endure,
and he was left behind to bear the mark.
My job was keeper, plainclothes guardian,
and model convert: stationed at his home,
I'd lead the tour groups over for a look
at him, Christ's greatest miracle so far,
then lead them out, careful to watch for signs
that marked them allies — traitors, possibly —
though most were only curious: fellow Jews
still on the fence, willing to be convinced.
He'd tear the bread, dip it in olive oil,
and chew — he'd chew so thoroughly, I'd want
to shake him by the sleeve, "Enough already!"
crumbs stuck in his beard, but turned away
instead to talk with those who watched, inspired.
The sisters, Martha and Mary, ran the house —
they, their servants, and some hangers-on —
what good could *he* do, wandering at will,
vanished for hours, sometimes on the day

he knew I'd show him off; I'd stall for time
with shepherds, moneylenders grown impatient
for the proof that we'd exchange for faith.
(I lost more than a few of them that way.)
Why him? What were we getting for the deal?
The rest of us, I felt, deserved some scrap
of what his afterlife, or lack of it,
had shown: the secrets he was holding back.
I thought of my dead wife, my only daughter,
a few more who'd have better suited me
to make the trip, if I'd had any say....
I didn't, and they haven't to this day.
Another week, another round of doubters,
lousy conversation, worst of all
the resurrected host's, and my small place
in Someone's great plan hidden from us all.
And then, the sideshow wrapped; the curtain closed.
Some said: Apostles' orders, others told
me that the Pharisees had placed a contract
on his head since he inspired belief,
having, you know, once come back from the dead.
Good luck the second time, I thought to say,
but checked myself: what was the latest Word,
brought back with loaves and palm-branch souvenirs?
He that hates his life here in this world
will live eternally. Did that explain
why Lazarus had grown so loathe to speak,
unnerving even those who loved him once —
Mary, who washed his feet and rubbed his joints,
Martha, who brewed the heavy lentil soup
in which he dipped his bread — and me, of course,
though love was not the feeling that I harbored.

Sometimes I think about the time I found him
standing off the road to Bethany,
some weed-choked precipice where I rushed forward,
grabbed his wrist and pulled him back to earth
to face our wrath, his duty, and the long
walk back. He answered "Nothing" every time
I asked what he'd been doing, what he saw.
Maybe it's good he kept us in the dark.
As lookout, go-fer, keeper of the Faith's
corporeal proof, now stuck with other tasks
essential to the Cause, I'm guaranteed,
whatever rage the dead man made me feel,
I'll know — as he will, too — eternal life.

Green Ghost

Supplies for Transogram's 1965 glow-in-the-dark board game included the title character (a plastic ghost-shaped spinner) and his progeny: twelve child-ghosts, each named for a shade of green.

The object of the game: a kind of quest.
Green Ghost must find his son somewhere concealed
inside one of the crypts the board contains.
Eleven brothers fill eleven more,
but they're diversions: only one, long hidden,
calls for rescue underneath Dad's doleful
ectoplasmic gaze. Give him a spin
till Green Ghost's supernatural roulette
ticks down to leave him pointing at one player —
you, perhaps — required to choose a Key,
unsure of which will fit into the lock
to free his long-sought son, which crypt he's in,
or why one child, among so many dead,
should hold a value greater than the rest.

The Case Against Standardized Testing

December 4, 1976, Brentwood, L.I.

It's strange to say, but I, too, once was beautiful,
and not so long ago as you might think,
at 17, on foot on Second Avenue
past the Legion hall, the water tower
sky-high, emblazoned with my hometown's name,
bleeding rust along its battered tank.
Having survived the blank interrogation
of the SAT, its bubbles blacked
by No. 2 lead pencils pressed too hard,
I headed home. What would my future hold?
My mother was in the hospital again —
bummer — and Dad was working "off the books,"
a plumber who'd lost our Blue Cross with his job,
collecting unemployment till the checks
ran out or he got caught, bills mounting up
with each wrong diagnosis. The air was cold,
December-still, my wool brown-plaid shirt-jacket
just enough to shelter me from freezing
on the trek. I breathed out, watched my breath.

Why had I put things off, taking the test
beside the last dregs of the college-bound
(if we were bound for anything but labor)
sweeping eraser-shreds from answer sheets
down to the school gym's brightly polished floor?
Fearful the test would prove high hopes were futile,

I felt strangely light, as if convinced
the day's work would resolve my doubts at last,
for good or ill. I passed the railway house
that still served as our gateway to Penn Station,
New York: city of crime and bankruptcy,
two hours by rail, a universe away.
Would I end up there? Upstate? Somewhere else?
I mused, still only half-aware of traffic
humming beyond the tracks when, at my back,
an unmarked van braked loudly, powder-blue
and windowless. The driver — lank-haired, bearded —
did a double-take, flashing a look —
of recognition? Rage? What was he yelling? —
as I turned by reflex, met his eyes,
and, in that instant, knew his whole intent.

It wasn't good, and yet, I made excuses —
he thought he knew me, I'd imagined it —
and yet, what fault of mine had drawn his gaze?
I kept on walking, though his van reversed
and gunned as I strode from the railroad lot
over the tracks past Herrick Real Estate,
toward Jack in the Box, keeping a steady pace.

The burgers' sweet stench spoiled the winter air;
the light was red, and he was caught behind
a few cars, though I thought I saw him watching —
shit! He must have seen me looking, too.
I turned the corner, passing Campbell's Bakery
where, on childhood Sundays after church,
my dad would order crullers in a box
secured by red-and-white peppermint string

that made it bounce, suspended from my hand
— strange what you think of when you're feeling scared.

What made the driver seem so venomous?
A dead end block I'd never walked was close
and, running parallel, the tree-lined byways
of a residential boulevard —
the so-called Brentwood Parkway, grandly named,
my usual route when travelling on foot.
Maybe the guy had somewhere else to be?
The light changed; traffic surged; the van flew past,
sped to the shoulder fifty yards ahead
and parked. Right in my path. I was in danger,
I was sure of it: he'd stopped beside
a wooded lot unsold and long neglected —
nobody was anywhere nearby.

Did I see Christmas lights, or blue and white
bulbs lit for Hanukkah on that gray day,
edging the eaves of homes secure and safe?
Time's up. I had to choose. The "parkway" lanes
were too close to the van, and through it all
I didn't dare break stride. *Think fast*, I thought,
and took the dead end, casually crossing
without changing speed, as if pretending
that I'd noticed nothing meant my stalker
wouldn't feel the need to follow yet.

On a cold December street where you're unknown,
pursued and cut off by an unmarked van
driven by Manson's double in a town
rightly suspicious of strangers, vans, and teens,

what should you do? You can't just yell for help
— nobody cares, no one will call the cops,
who'd never show up in time, and if you run,
you can't outrun the van that's after you.
That's why, though I was certain it would fail,
I rang the bell of some neat bungalow,
hoping a Good Samaritan would answer,
hear me out, and offer sanctuary.
The front door swinging inward, storm door locked
between us, a woman eyed me, dubious.
I voiced my fear then asked to use her phone?
With one word, "No!" I felt the door bang shut,
stranding me on that well-kept dead end street
whose other residents would do the same,
if home at all. What now? Mr. Blue Van
might still give up, I hoped, more jerk than psycho
in search of someone new to prey upon,
some clueless teen to frighten till, amused,
he'd race off, feeling great. Or was he watching
from the same place where I'd seen him last,
ready to zoom up after me, and strike?

The dead end street led only one way: back —
but I could trick him if I cut across
the wooded yards of Brentwood Parkway's homes,
pine-shaded, built before the postwar boom,
instead of heading back the way I came.
Obscured by house and hedge, hoping to glimpse
somebody who could help, I took my chance
when, suddenly, there it was again: the van
tearing down Brentwood Parkway, past the trees,
the winter lawns, my own physician's shingle,

me (unseen), a powder-blue flash barreling
south from where he'd hoped to block my way,
back to the same lot where he'd first pulled over
— this meant he never saw the Dead End sign
but sped to where he thought the roads would join,
saw his mistake, and overshot his prey.

And maybe that's why I'm still here today
to talk about how beautiful I was,
though no more beautiful than you who listen
are, or once were, like the rest of us.
Besides, what's beauty next to the allure
of helplessness or youth that trips some wire
in those who prey on others, break their flesh
because they can, whatever the excuse?
I eluded my would-be captor, or whatever
he'd have proved himself, knocked on a door
closer to home, though every blur of motion
on the road, by then, looked powder-blue.
A woman kind to strangers let me use
her kitchen phone. I dialed my good friend Anna,
patient listener, to whom I poured
my shame — yes, it was shame, relief, and fear
I felt, though none are words I would've used,
voice quavering, falsely brave.
I got home safe,
and lived to see my high school marching band,
our "Green Machine," the pride of New York State,
laden with brass and drums, confetti-blind
in Jimmy Carter's inaugural parade,
undaunted by cold or January wind.
Beside my mom recuperating slowly

on her bed, I watched, self-doubting teen
(Is there another kind?) whose memory held
a few short years, a lifetime, an escape —
my dad's post-bakery missions to the deli
for Lucky Strikes and, for his wife and son,
the *Sunday News* wrapped in Dick Tracy, Dondi,
and their kin before we headed home.
Home — where safety was, and family dwelled,
where no one could intrude through doors shut tight,
where memory was shaped — the future, too.
What would mine hold? Would it be worth the wait?
I couldn't know...
                    But all that lay ahead
depended on that walk home when a test
booked on my future ex-wife's fifteenth birthday
brought me, guileless, to a time and place
when every choice was weighed, for good or ill,
its decades-long unfolding still unseen —
What would her life have held if I'd been caught?
less joy, I want to think, less sorrow I know —
and home's elusive, only an empty house
where shelter from the near dark welcomes you.

On Goodbyes

I hate goodbyes. I don't mean those we dread,
foresee or bring about, that shadow us,
but those that take us by surprise, the dead

air empty in their wake. The words are less
important than that someone cuts the cord
quickly: so much already shadows us

we dare invite no more, no single word
or phrase beyond a short *God-be-with-you,*
Farewell, Good Night. We want to reach accord

cleanly, without rancor, then cut through
the crowd, escape, forget. Speak soon enough,
before someone can say "goodbye" to you,

or else, you'll watch it happen, hear the laugh
meant kindly, simulated through the noise
of crowds still trapped, not leaving fast enough

to drown the false cheer carried in a voice.
The need to part is real. The words are noise.
I hate goodbyes: from those — to those — we dread
and need, who take or leave us, like the dead.

Already Seen/Always Seen

We call it déjà vu, "already seen,"
the past encroaching falsely on the present,
Then on Now, recovered memory
provoked by some return — a real one, maybe,
to some routine crossroads or abode —
or, likelier, a false one based on nothing
more than mere resemblance, seen again.
The instant that we feel it — act or place
abruptly, unexpectedly familiar,
what we hear no chance remark but language
bearing some elusive resonance
originating in an absent past —
what else do we remember, passing through —
dismayed, elated — as it fades from view?

But, more, what do we call the other feeling
when the world we live in every day
recedes, our loved ones' voices turned to murmurs
indistinct, our own fallen away,
half-overheard, at best? What is the feeling
when the past, more urgent than the present,
presses forward to exact attention
from the world that holds our real lives?
To feel the past's more present than the Now,
the Soon-to-Come Reward, or what-you-will,
is to concede that everything we hear
is only noise, faint shadows closing in
that fade in fast retreat, as shadows do,
the treasured past more visible, more true.

Holy Wars for Us

No Holy Wars for them; the most the small
Can ever give us is a nuisance brawl.
— Robert Frost, "No Holy Wars for Them"

Frost's world is gone, if it was ever here.
States strong enough to do good bring, instead,
more wrong than he imagined. Every year,
they offer threats designed to silence dread
(nothing restores the confidence they've lost),
and brute force — self-perpetuating, vast.
Frost, are you listening? Those states too small
break into tribes that rise up in a rage
of bloodshed that won't stop. The nuisance brawl
is sneak attack and murder, ancient page
and verse updated to record the crimes
that add up, death by death, to countless lifetimes.
The great lose ground. What should they guard it with?
Real bombs explode all rhetoric and myth.

Graduation Day

June 1, 2013, Towson High School, Maryland;
For my step-daughter Catherine, and for Jane

Even before the mortarboards explode
over the girls in white, the boys in red
back in their rows, two dozen county banners
brightening the stage, the tiered arena

packed with parents, guardians, and grans,
my wife's — your mother's — eyes well at the thought
of all that lies before you, all that's past.
How can I help? I know just what she's thinking:

Here you are, your march across the stage
already over, restless with your classmates
during speeches shorter than we'd feared,
and in your hands, forgotten, the diploma

that will mark your crossing from our lives.
What do you carry in your memory?
The flight from Britain in a Fulbright year
that ended with your birth? Your parents' divorce,

shared custody, the strain of their divide
for eighteen years and more? And now, in line,
you patiently endure the last few words
of benediction soon to cue the instant

when you turn your tassel.... What did you
discover on your rides home through the years,
court-ordered, counted in the pre-dawn light?
Your mother sees you as you were back then,

and as you are today, transformed by time:
white-robed, like all the girls in your row
a dozen yards below us on the floor
below the stage, standing expectantly.

They see — not us, who occupied a place
like theirs, nor teachers stationed on the stage,
whose handshakes move the graduates along
grinning, to cheers and whoops and wild applause.

No, what they see are flashes of themselves,
too brief to hold, projected on a scrim
of "dreams" — a word we've heard too much today,
in song and valediction.... Still in tune

despite exertions on the overture
that welcomed us, your high school orchestra
selects its swan song from a makeshift pit
below the podium; the tassels turn

in unison (almost), three hundred smooth
hands, steady, youthful, twisting right to left
the plaited threads that serve as metaphor
of thresholds crossed, deeds done; and I remember,

both before and after, how you clasped
your mother's hand, not yet tall as her shoulder
as you turned, teeth wired, gold hair tied back,
and asked, as you were leaving my apartment,

if I'd still hold on to it when married
to your mother so we still could gather
on this high floor over Baltimore,
the skyline visible, green lawns below,

to eat ice cream and nod off to some movie
while my black cat watched us skeptically…
We laughed but knew what you were getting at:
How would your own life change when I moved in?

— Step-child and almost-daughter, borrowed briefly,
only to be relinquished to a world
where, soon enough, you'll find a lasting place,
as I did, by your mother's side, I wish you

more than I can say. The storm of caps
goes flying upward — soon, the brass will sound,
strings, drums, and woodwinds running to catch up,
tired families heading home — but as they fall,

caps hurled so fast we hardly saw them fly,
some trampled accidentally on the floor,
I touch your mother's hand as if to bear
away some portion of the loss we share,

and feel her joy as well: to see her daughter —
you, the child who should have been our own —
vows sworn, achievements praised, and speeches done,
delivered to this day and all to come.

Stray Crow

Once, long ago, I played the rescuer
to your lost kin, stray crow. Not ten years old,
I found a soaked near-drowned bird in the filter
of our pool. Is water memory,

the flood that bears us, stunned, into what's next?
If so, then I'm surprised that we're so calm,
one of us having flown, somehow, through time:
some cosmic rip intangible, yet near —

It must be you, because I'm all grown up
and you're still black, bright black, like polished stone
layered, engraved. You're grounded, but alive,

and if you had the power of speech, would you
bring news of that boy or, perhaps, his father
who removed you, saved, till you took flight?

Today, I find you, tail askew, successor
or original, where you took shelter
after storms, now hobbled. Stairwell dweller
towel-caught, eyeing movement through the weave

and basket lid, you glimpse my wife (she drives
us to the Rescue in her stalwart Saturn,
having traveled time to be with me
and save you, too). What joins us is some pattern

no one knows, that prints its secret text
upon our lives…And when the sign appears,
a flaming phoenix, nailed to a post,

I know I'm in the present, not the past
from which you flew, stray crow, the ride uphill,
sun-crossed, leaf-shaded, heading into light.

Upcycling Paumanok

The dream that drove the development of Long Island is no longer viable….

— Long Island Index/Rauch Foundation
Press Release, Garden City,
October 4, 2010

Into a future no one can foresee
we look again: the time is now, past now,
to Build a Better Burb — resounding catch phrase

of the Rauch Foundation's urgent call
to artists, architects, and city planners:
Save Long Island! Rescue Paumanok!

from history and itself. Design is all,
so Simons, Cobb, and Lovett offer theirs:
"Upcycling 2.0," a plan requiring

what we throw away to serve some purpose,
trash not just recycled but improved,
suburbia changed, transformed to paradise.

It won't just happen. Vision is required.
There must be vistas, open land unfolding —
planted, planned, an aerial view pristine,

wind-turbines poking from an azure ocean
acid-free, a clear sky shimmering;
and, yes, we'll need new housing, public space,

car-free mobility, and access to
essential services. Walt Whitman glimpsed
on far horizons riches, mystery,

eternal progress; I myself have seen
his birthplace and his mall not half a mile
apart, and both have served in different ways

as art and commerce: upcycling's domain.
In paintings that depict the project's aims,
the atmosphere is sobering. Such light —

morning or afternoon? It's hard to tell,
gray streets swept clean of traffic, untouched roads
to Paumanok's twin forks on time's long trip;

and trailing every image is the jargon
that defines it: "Vertical Integration,"
"Incremental Renewal," and the like,

though I like best the proudly pennywise
"Pooled Income Stream for Public Benefit" —
Translation: *Want a future? Pay for it.*

I get it, and I truly hope it works,
though such ambitions leave me skeptical.
Will vendors sell organic vegetables

on roads turned "agricultural corridors"?
Will water towers scaled down to fit in parks
shade those who stroll beneath, as in this concept

architects propose? Who'll build these homes
upcycled into perfect neighborhoods,
function and form united, one at last?

Upcycling's seers, Columbia students all,
will split a cash prize, like the other teams
whose grand designs make sport of future shock,

to please the judges' politics or eye.
— and yet, I find myself drawn back to paintings
that define the project's perfect circle —

nothing wasted, discord harmonized —
as if I could walk into any image
that I choose and join the shadows there,

shadows that might be us, but aren't yet,
calmly gathered, sprawled out for the next
outdoor performance by a few more shadows

guaranteed not to be overrun
by shades left homeless (no one's homeless here);
collectively composting, as directed,

near constructions always painted white,
bleached surfaces awaiting text or touch
from silhouettes who walk this tranquil space,

transparent as ghosts or wisps of smoke.... Are we
the generations Whitman once foresaw?
I think about his mall, futurist vision

half a century old, now obsolete,
repeatedly renovated, incomplete
was it that long ago I glanced up, dazzled

by its ceiling that seemed miles away,
where one balloon held still? Life, Whitman wrote,
comes rising to the surface in upheaval —

airships dangled, weightless, in the skies
once, long ago; ships broke free of their berths,
invulnerable ocean liners rumbling

through gray mist. They carried shadows, too.
Like them, we've no idea what world will follow,
when we, too, are claimed for some new purpose,

sadly, joyfully. Who'll be reborn?
Step forward; take my hand: and on the day
our lost past surfaces, we'll walk on streets

eternal like ourselves, all debts in balance,
wrongs forgiven, wasted lives reclaimed,
the only shadows left the ones we cast.

For the Next-to-Last Survivor

For Barbara West Dainton (1911-2007), at the time of her death, one of the Titanic's last two living survivors

In Lifeboat 10, you leave the ill-starred ship
listing below the iceberg's greenish light,
all decks in chaos, North Atlantic night
scattered with stars, auroral. Sound asleep
moments ago, but now a daughter pressed
helplessly to her mother — saved, somehow,
unlike so many — what will you recall,
a ten-month-old whose father, scrubbed and dressed,
waves farewell from this foundering? Like snow,
ice flakes and ash blow past your face and fall,
melting, on silk.
                        But one day, in a future
inconceivable, you'll flee once more,
this time alone, transformed impossibly —
your passing mourned, but not the last to be.

Notes

The epigraph of "Ouija for Beginners" is from nineteenth-century advertisements for the Ouija Board by William Fuld, who popularized the manufactured version.

"The *Poseidon*, Capsized": *The Poseidon Adventure* (1972) was directed by Ronald Neame and disaster-movie mogul Irwin Allen; Wendell Mayes and Stirling Silliphant adapted Paul Gallico's novel for the screen. W. T. Grant's, a so-called "five-and-dime" department store established in 1906, grew to a national chain but failed in 1976 in what was then the second largest bankruptcy in American history.

In this era, seventh- to ninth-graders in Long Island public schools attended a "junior high," then entered high school for grades ten through twelve.

The "Aerial Views of Levittown" may be seen online in the context of Peter Bacon Hales' article "Levittown: Documents of an Ideal American Suburb." Hale concludes, "That [Levittown's] history contains the paradoxes and failures of the American Dream, including racial covenants in the early Levitt-controlled years, only serves to remind us of its dependence on the deepest streams of American culture, both noble and ignoble."

A key source for "Snow in Baghdad" is the January 11, 2008 *Associated Press* report "Many Baghdad Residents See Snow for the First Time," carried online and in print by various outlets.

The epigraph of "Rondel for a Timepiece Not Yet Obsolete" is from Susan Lee's "Are wristwatches becoming obsolete?" (*Columbia News Service*, December 27, 2005).

"For Jacob Kurtzburg": Information on the life and career of comics giant Jack Kirby is drawn from *The Comics Journal Library, Volume One: Jack Kirby* (Fantagraphics Books, 2002), especially "Interview I: 'There is something stupid in violence as violence'" (conducted by Mark Hebert) and "Interview II: 'I created an army of characters, and now my connection with them is lost'" (conducted by Tim Skelly). Kirby co-created Captain America with Joe Simon prior to the U.S. entry into WWII.

Kirby's collaborator and editor during the 1960's (and co-creator of the Marvel Universe) was Stan Lee. The poem's "fallen angel" is the Silver Surfer, herald of world-devouring Galactus.

Sources for "Times Square Post Cards" include Jack H. Smith's *Old New York in Picture Post Cards 1900-1945* (Vestal Press, 1999) and Rod Kennedy, Jr.'s *Lost New York in Old Postcards* (Gibbs Smith, 2001).

Sources for "Return to Slumberland" include *The Best of Little Nemo in Slumberland*, edited by Richard Marshchall (Stewart, Tabori, and Chang, 1997).

"Breakthrough"'s epigraph is from Sharon Begley's "Mind Reading Is Now Possible," *Newsweek*, January 21, 2008.

The John's Bargain Store mentioned in "The Woods" was a well-known New York area chain of the mid- to late '60s that sold cheap clothes and manufacturers' overstock in an ever-changing, fairly random sampling.

"Holy Wars for Us": Robert Frost's "No Holy Wars for Them" appears in *The Poetry of Robert Frost*, edited by Edward Connery Lathem (Holt, Rinehart, and Winston, 1969).

"Upcycling Paumanok": From the Long Island Index/Rauch Foundation Press Release (Garden City, March 31, 2010) announcing the Build a Better Burb ideas competition (the words quoted are those of Nancy Rauch Douzinas): "'The postwar "first" suburbs, exemplified nationwide by Long Island's own Levittown, are now pushing sixty years old and the needs of these communities have changed dramatically over the years. Now is the moment to address contemporary challenges by retrofitting the prewar suburban landscape of small towns and train transit that languished during decades of construction of new highways, shopping malls, gated subdivisions, and far-flung office parks.'"

The October 4, 2010 winners' press release includes this follow-up: "A distinguished panel of jurors selected 23 finalists and then 6 winners from entries submitted by architects, urban designers, planners, visionaries and students, all vying for $22,500 in prizes." Upcycling 2.0 was designed by Columbia University Graduate School of Architecture, Planning and Preservation students Ryan H. B. Lovett, John B. Simons, and Patrick Cobb.

The Walt Whitman Mall's grand opening ceremony was held on November 23, 1962. Less than half a mile away is the Walt Whitman Birthplace State Historic Site and Interpretive Center.

The Author

Ned Balbo's *The Trials of Edgar Poe and Other Poems* received the Poets' Prize and the Donald Justice Prize. His second book, *Lives of the Sleepers*, was awarded the Ernest Sandeen Prize and a *ForeWord* Book of the Year Gold Medal. *Galileo's Banquet,* his first volume, shared the Towson University Prize. The recipient of three Maryland Arts Council grants, the Robert Frost Foundation Poetry Award, and co-winner of the Willis Barnstone Translation Prize, he has held fellowships or residencies at the Sewanee Writers' Conference, the Vermont Studio Center, and the Virginia Center for the Creative Arts.

His poetry, prose, and translations appear in print or online at *American Life in Poetry*, *Cimarron Review*, *Creative Nonfiction*, *Hopkins Review*, *Iowa Review*, *New Criterion*, *Pleiades*, *The Poetry Foundation* website, *Shenandoah*, *Sou'wester*, *Writer's Almanac*, *Verse Daily*, and elsewhere. Anthology appearances include work in the Everyman's Library volumes *Villanelles* and *Monster Verse: Poems Human and Inhuman* (Knopf), *Air Fare: Stories, Poems, and Essays on Flight* (Sarabande), and *Drawn to Marvel: poems from the comic books* (Minor Arcana).

Balbo holds degrees from Vassar College, the Writing Seminars at Johns Hopkins, and the Iowa Writers' Workshop. He is married to poet-essayist Jane Satterfield and currently teaches in the MFA program in Creative Writing and Environment at Iowa State University.

www.ingramcontent.com/pod-product-compliance
Lightning Source LLC
Chambersburg PA
CBHW030428310726
48979CB00009B/1662/J

* 9 7 8 1 9 3 9 5 7 4 1 5 2 *